W9-CFC-028

DATE DUE

21st Century
Basic Skills
Library

KEEPING COOL IN SUMMER

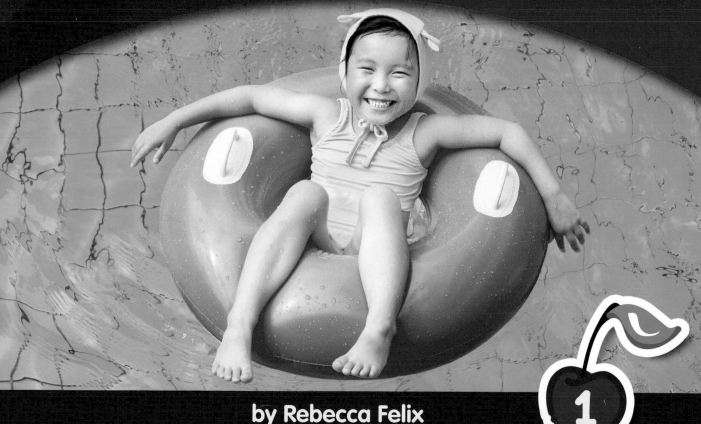

by Rebecca Felix

Cherry Lake Publishing • Ann Arbor, Michigan

1

Published in the United States of America
by Cherry Lake Publishing
Ann Arbor, Michigan
www.cherrylakepublishing.com

Consultant: Marla Conn, ReadAbility, Inc.
Editorial direction and book production: Red Line Editorial

Photo Credits: Tom Wang/Shutterstock Images, cover, 1; Comstock/
Stockbyte/Thinkstock, 4, 12; Patrick Foto/Shutterstock Images, 6; Terry J
Alcorn/iStock/Thinkstock, 8; Bloomimage/Corbis, 10; suksao999/iStock/
Thinkstock, 14; Rob Marmion/Shutterstock Images, 16; Stuart Monk/
Shutterstock Images, 18; Pressmaster/Shutterstock Images, 20

Library of Congress Cataloging-in-Publication Data
Felix, Rebecca, 1984- author.
  Keeping cool in summer / by Rebecca Felix.
    pages cm. -- (Let's look at summer)
  Audience: Age 6.
  Audience: Grades K to 3.
  Includes index.
  ISBN 978-1-63137-597-2 (hardcover) -- ISBN 978-1-63137-642-9 (pbk.)
-- ISBN 978-1-63137-687-0 (pdf ebook) -- ISBN 978-1-63137-732-7 (hosted
ebook)
  1. Body temperature--Regulation--Juvenile literature. 2. Human
physiology--Juvenile literature. 3. Summer--Juvenile literature. 4. Heat--
Juvenile literature. I. Title.

QP135.F45 2013
612.01426--dc23

                                    2014004448

Cherry Lake Publishing would like to acknowledge the work of The
Partnership for 21st Century Skills. Please visit www.p21.org for more
information.

Printed in the United States of America
Corporate Graphics Inc.
July 2014

TABLE OF CONTENTS

Heat

Summer is hot. How do people keep cool?

What Do You See?

Where is the shade?

6

Jen sits in the **shade**. It blocks the sun's hot **rays**.

Sweat

People **sweat**. It makes skin wet. We feel cooler as it dries.

Air

Fans move air. Moving air dries sweat. This helps us feel cool.

Air conditioners blow cool air. They keep buildings cool.

What Do You See?

What is Abby holding?

Water

Abby swims. Pool water is cooler than her skin. It cools her down.

What Do You See?

What is on Ren's head?

Ren swims in cool ocean water.

Kai drinks water. **Hydrated** bodies keep cool better.

Treats

Ava eats ice cream. It makes her feel cool. What other summer treats are cold?

Find Out More

BOOK
Llewellyn, Claire. *A Cool Summer*. New York: Oxford UP, 2011.

WEB SITE
How to Be Safe When You're in the Sun—KidsHealth
kidshealth.org/kid/watch/out/summer_safety.html#
Read about ways to stay safe and cool in the summer sun.

Glossary

hydrated (HYE-drayt-id) supplied with enough water
rays (RAYZ) thin beams of light from the sun
shade (SHAYD) a place where hot sunlight is blocked
sweat (SWET) when moisture comes through skin

Home and School Connection

Use this list of words from the book to help your child become a better reader. Word games and writing activities can help beginning readers reinforce literacy skills.

air conditioners	dries	hydrated	shade
blocks	drinks	ice cream	sits
blow	eats	keep	skin
bodies	fans	makes	summer
buildings	feel	move	sun
cold	head	moving	sweat
cool	heat	ocean	swims
cooler	helps	people	treats
down	holding	pool	water
	hot	rays	wet

What Do You See?

What Do You See? is a feature paired with select photos in this book. It encourages young readers to interact with visual images in order to build the ability to integrate content in various media formats.

You can help your child further evaluate photos in this book with additional activities. Look at the images in the book without the What Do You See? feature. Ask your child to describe one detail in each image, such as a food, activity, or setting.

23

Index

About the Author

Rebecca Felix is an editor and writer from Minnesota. Summers there are hot. Rebecca keeps cool in summer by swimming in pools and eating ice cream!